Better Homes and Gardens.

Cookies & Cakes

Easy Everyday Recipe Library

BETTER HOMES AND GARDENS® BOOKS
Des Moines, Iowa

EASY EVERYDAY RECIPE LIBRARY

Better Homes and Gardens® Books, An imprint of Meredith® Books
Published for Creative World Enterprises LP, West Chester, Pennsylvania
www.creativeworldcooking.com

Cookies & Cakes

Project Editors: Spectrum Communication Services, Inc.
Project Designers: Seif Visual Communications
Copy Chief: Catherine Hamrick
Copy and Production Editor: Terri Fredrickson
Contributing Proofreaders: Kathy Eastman, Susan J. Kling
Electronic Production Coordinator: Paula Forest
Editorial and Design Assistants: Judy Bailey, Mary Lee Gavin, Karen Schirm
Test Kitchen Director: Lynn Blanchard
Production Director: Douglas M. Johnston
Production Managers: Pam Kvitne, Marjorie J. Schenkelberg

Meredith® Books
Editor in Chief: James D. Blume
Design Director: Matt Strelecki
Managing Editor: Gregory H. Kayko

Director, Sales & Marketing, Retail: Michael A. Peterson
Director, Sales & Marketing, Special Markets: Rita McMullen
Director, Sales & Marketing, Home & Garden Center Channel: Ray Wolf
Director, Operations: George A. Susral

Vice President, General Manager: Jamie L. Martin

Better Homes and Gardens® Magazine
Editor in Chief: Jean LemMon
Executive Food Editor: Nancy Byal

Meredith Publishing Group
President, Publishing Group: Christopher M. Little
Vice President, Consumer Marketing & Development: Hal Oringer

Meredith Corporation
Chairman and Chief Executive Officer: William T. Kerr

Chairman of the Executive Committee: E. T. Meredith III

Creative World Enterprises LP
Publisher: Richard J. Petrone
Design Consultants to Creative World Enterprises: Coastline Studios, Orlando, Florida

All of us at Better Homes and Gardens® Books are dedicated to providing you with the information and ideas you need to create delicious foods. We welcome your comments and suggestions. Write to us at: Better Homes and Gardens Books, Cookbook Editorial Department, 1716 Locust St., Des Moines, Iowa 50309-3023.

Our seal assures you that every recipe in *Cookies & Cakes* has been tested in the Better Homes and Gardens® Test Kitchen. This means that each recipe is practical and reliable, and meets our high standards of taste appeal. We guarantee your satisfaction with this book for as long as you own it.

Cover photo: Ultimate Bar Cookies (see recipe, page 15) and Creamy, Fudgy, Nutty Brownies (see recipe, page 16)

Mmmm…there's nothing quite like the enticing aroma
of warm cookies or a freshly baked cake.

Quiet your cookie cravings with homemade nut cookies, zesty
spice cookies, or deep, rich chocolate cookies. Chewy and crisp,
big and small, you'll find the ultimate cookies to serve family
and friends. And browsing through our selection of cakes is like
touring your favorite bakery. We have easy-fixin' snack cakes,
velvet-crumbed layer cakes, and a feather-light angel food cake.

So come on! Savor the flavors and the sweet tastes
of success with these sensational recipes.

CONTENTS

White-Chocolate-Raspberry Cookies

If it's your turn to host the block party or the Christmas party, try these handsome melt-in-your-mouth cookies. They're elegant and sophisticated enough to serve as a simple dessert.

8 ounces white baking bars
½ cup butter
1 cup sugar
1 teaspoon baking soda
¼ teaspoon salt
2 eggs
2¾ cups all-purpose flour
½ cup seedless raspberry jam
3 ounces white baking bars
½ teaspoon shortening

Grease a cookie sheet. Set aside. Chop 4 ounces of the white baking bars. Set aside. In a heavy small saucepan heat another 4 ounces of the white baking bars over low heat till melted, stirring constantly; cool.

In a large mixing bowl beat butter with an electric mixer on medium to high speed for 30 seconds. Add the sugar, baking soda, and salt; beat till combined. Beat in the eggs and melted white baking bars till combined. Beat in as much of the flour as you can with the mixer. Stir in the remaining flour. Stir in the 4 ounces chopped white baking bars.

Drop dough by a rounded teaspoon about 2 inches apart onto the prepared cookie sheet. Bake in a 375° oven for 7 to 9 minutes or till edges are lightly browned. Cool on cookie sheet for 1 minute. Transfer to a wire rack; cool.

Just before serving, in a small saucepan heat the raspberry jam over low heat till melted. Spoon about ½ teaspoon jam onto the top of each cookie.

In a heavy small saucepan combine the 3 ounces white baking bars and shortening. Heat over low heat till melted, stirring constantly. Drizzle over cookies. If necessary, chill about 15 minutes to firm baking bar mixture. Makes about 48 cookies.

Nutrition information per cookie: 104 calories, 1 g protein, 16 g carbohydrate, 4 g fat (2 g saturated), 14 mg cholesterol, 66 mg sodium.

Toasted Oatmeal Cookies

Give your old-fashioned iced oatmeal cookies a nutty richness by browning the rolled oats slightly in the oven before using. If you like, toast a batch of oatmeal ahead and keep it on hand in an airtight container.

1½ cups regular rolled oats
⅓ cup buttermilk or sour milk
2 cups packed brown sugar
¾ cup shortening
1 teaspoon baking powder
1 teaspoon baking soda
1 teaspoon ground cinnamon
1 teaspoon ground nutmeg
½ teaspoon salt
2 eggs
1 teaspoon vanilla
2½ cups all-purpose flour
1 cup chopped pitted dates
1 cup chopped walnuts or pecans
Powdered Sugar Icing (optional)

Spread the oats in a shallow baking pan. Bake in a 375° oven about 10 minutes or till lightly toasted, stirring once. Meanwhile, grease a cookie sheet.

Place toasted oats in a small bowl. Stir in buttermilk or sour milk and let stand a few minutes.

In a medium mixing bowl beat together the brown sugar and shortening with an electric mixer on medium to high speed till combined. Add the baking powder, baking soda, cinnamon, nutmeg, and salt; beat till combined. Beat in the eggs and vanilla. Beat in the oat mixture.

Beat in as much of the flour as you can with the mixer. Stir in the remaining flour, dates, and nuts. Drop dough by a rounded teaspoon about 2 inches apart onto the prepared cookie sheet.

Bake in the 375° oven about 10 minutes or till edges are golden brown. Transfer cookies to a wire rack; cool. If desired, drizzle with Powdered Sugar Icing. Makes about 60 cookies.

Powdered Sugar Icing: In a small bowl combine 1 cup sifted *powdered sugar* and ¼ teaspoon *vanilla*. Stir in enough *milk* (2 to 4 teaspoons) to make an icing of drizzling consistency.

Nutrition information per cookie: 100 calories, 1 g protein, 15 g carbohydrate, 4 g fat (1 g saturated), 7 mg cholesterol, 52 mg sodium.

Malted Milk Cookies

You'll be reminded of a creamy old-fashioned malt every time you take a bite of these chocolate cookies.

1 cup butter
¾ cup granulated sugar
¾ cup packed brown sugar
1 teaspoon baking soda
2 eggs
2 ounces unsweetened chocolate, melted and cooled
1 teaspoon vanilla
2¼ cups all-purpose flour
½ cup instant malted milk powder
1 cup coarsely chopped malted milk balls

In a large mixing bowl beat the butter with an electric mixer on medium to high speed for 30 seconds. Add the granulated sugar, brown sugar, and baking soda. Beat the mixture till combined, scraping the sides of the bowl occasionally.

Beat in the eggs, melted chocolate, and vanilla till combined. Beat in as much of the flour as you can with the mixer. Stir in the remaining flour and the malted milk powder. Stir in the malted milk balls.

Drop dough by a rounded teaspoon about 2½ inches apart onto an ungreased cookie sheet. Bake in a 375° oven about 10 minutes or till edges are firm.

Cool on cookie sheet for 1 minute. Transfer cookies to a wire rack; cool. Makes about 36 cookies.

Nutrition information per cookie: 138 calories, 2 g protein, 18 g carbohydrate, 7 g fat (4 g saturated), 26 mg cholesterol, 112 mg sodium.

Margarine in Baking

The recipes in this book call for butter, not margarine, because it ensures the best results. Although baked goods made with some margarines can be satisfactory, choosing the right margarine is tricky. Many margarines contain more water than oil, which will yield undesirable results. If you choose to use margarine, select a stick margarine that lists at least 80 percent vegetable oil or 100 calories per tablespoon on the package. Diet, whipped, liquid, and soft spreads or margarines are for table use—not baking. Their high water content can make baked goods wet and tough.

Chocolate Chip Cookies

Nothing beats a classic. Chocolate chip cookies were probably the first cookies you ever baked. This recipe is an updated version that first appeared in the 1941 edition of the Better Homes and Gardens® cookbook.

½ cup shortening
½ cup butter
1 cup packed brown sugar
½ cup granulated sugar
½ teaspoon baking soda
2 eggs
1 teaspoon vanilla
2½ cups all-purpose flour
1 12-ounce package (2 cups) semisweet chocolate pieces
1½ cups chopped walnuts, pecans, or hazelnuts (filberts) (optional)

In a large mixing bowl beat the shortening and butter with an electric mixer on medium to high speed for 30 seconds. Add the brown sugar, granulated sugar, and baking soda. Beat the mixture till combined, scraping the sides of the bowl occasionally.

Beat in the eggs and vanilla till combined. Beat in as much of the flour as you can with the mixer. Stir in the remaining flour. Stir in the chocolate pieces and, if desired, the chopped nuts.

Drop dough by a rounded teaspoon about 2 inches apart onto an ungreased cookie sheet.

Bake in a 375° oven for 8 to 10 minutes or till edges are lightly browned. Transfer cookies to a wire rack; cool. Makes about 60 cookies.

Nutrition information per cookie: 93 calories, 1 g protein, 12 g carbohydrate, 5 g fat (1 g saturated), 11 mg cholesterol, 29 mg sodium.

Frosted Sour Cream-Chocolate Drops

These deep chocolate delights—topped with a chocolate-butter cream frosting—are just too tempting. So that they don't disappear all at once, you might want to store some out of sight.

½ cup butter
1 cup packed brown sugar
½ teaspoon baking soda
¼ teaspoon salt
1 8-ounce carton dairy sour cream
1 egg
2 ounces unsweetened chocolate, melted and cooled
1 teaspoon vanilla
2 cups all-purpose flour
Chocolate Butter Frosting

In a large mixing bowl beat butter with an electric mixer on medium to high speed for 30 seconds. Add brown sugar, baking soda, and salt. Beat till combined, scraping sides of bowl occasionally. Beat in the sour cream, egg, melted chocolate, and vanilla till combined. Beat in as much of the flour as you can with the mixer. Stir in the remaining flour.

Drop dough by a slightly rounded teaspoon about 3 inches apart onto an ungreased cookie sheet. Bake in a 350° oven for 8 to 10 minutes or till edges are firm.

Transfer cookies to a wire rack; cool. Spread the cooled cookies with Chocolate Butter Frosting. Makes about 42 cookies.

Chocolate Butter Frosting: In a medium mixing bowl beat ¼ cup *butter* till fluffy. Gradually add 1 cup sifted *powdered sugar* and ⅓ cup unsweetened *cocoa powder*, beating well. Gradually beat in 3 tablespoons *milk* and 1 teaspoon *vanilla*. Gradually beat in 1½ cups additional sifted *powdered sugar*. If necessary, beat in additional *milk* to make of spreading consistency.

Nutrition information per cookie: 111 calories, 1 g protein, 15 g carbohydrate, 5 g fat (3 g saturated), 16 mg cholesterol, 67 mg sodium.

Fudge Ecstasies

You'll think you broke the chocolate bank when you bite into one of these chewy, double-chocolate, nut-filled wonders.

1   12-ounce package (2 cups)
      semisweet chocolate pieces
2   ounces unsweetened chocolate,
      chopped
2   tablespoons butter
2   eggs
⅔   cup sugar
¼   cup all-purpose flour
1   teaspoon vanilla
¼   teaspoon baking powder
1   cup chopped nuts

Grease a cookie sheet. Set aside. In a heavy medium saucepan combine 1 cup of the chocolate pieces, the unsweetened chocolate, and butter. Cook and stir over medium-low heat till melted. Remove from heat.

Add the eggs, sugar, flour, vanilla, and baking powder. Beat till combined, scraping sides of pan occasionally. Stir in the remaining chocolate pieces and the nuts.

Drop dough by a rounded teaspoon about 2 inches apart onto prepared cookie sheet. Bake in a 350° oven for 8 to 10 minutes or till edges are firm and surfaces are dull and slightly cracked. Transfer to a wire rack; cool. Makes about 36 cookies.

Nutrition information per cookie: 101 calories, 2 g protein, 12 g carbohydrate, 6 g fat (1 g saturated), 14 mg cholesterol, 13 mg sodium.

Getting Cookie Yields Right

Does your actual cookie count come up short when you check it against the yield listed in the recipe? If so, you're probably using too much dough per cookie. To drop dough by rounded teaspoons, use spoons from your flatware set (not measuring spoons or flatware soup or serving spoons). The dough should fill the spoon and mound slightly to give a nicely rounded top. If you prefer larger cookies, scoop a little more dough onto the spoon and allow 1 to 2 minutes more baking time. Just remember, you'll wind up with fewer cookies.

Oatmeal Jumbos

Make these cookies large or small. Both sizes are big in peanut butter and chocolate taste.

1 cup peanut butter
½ cup butter
1½ cups packed brown sugar
½ cup granulated sugar
1½ teaspoons baking powder
½ teaspoon baking soda
3 eggs
2 teaspoons vanilla
4 cups rolled oats
1½ cups candy-coated milk chocolate pieces
¾ cup chopped peanuts, walnuts, or pecans

In a large mixing bowl beat peanut butter and butter with an electric mixer on medium to high speed for 30 seconds. Add the brown sugar, granulated sugar, baking powder, and baking soda; beat till combined.

Beat in the eggs and vanilla till combined. Stir in the rolled oats. Stir in the candy-coated milk chocolate pieces and nuts.

Drop dough by a ¼-cup measure or scoop about 4 inches apart onto an ungreased cookie sheet. Bake in a 350° oven about 15 minutes or till edges are lightly browned.

(Or, for small cookies, drop dough by a rounded teaspoon about 2 inches apart onto an ungreased cookie sheet. Bake in a 350° oven about 10 minutes.)

Cool for 1 minute on the cookie sheet. Transfer the cookies to a wire rack; cool. Makes about 26 large or about 60 small cookies.

Nutrition information per large cookie: 272 calories, 7 g protein, 32 g carbohydrate, 14 g fat (4 g saturated), 34 mg cholesterol, 173 mg sodium.

Fall Fruit Drops

If you haven't used hickory nuts, give them a try in this fruit-filled cookie. Hickory nuts have a rich, buttery flavor.

⅔ cup golden raisins, snipped dried apricots, and/or chopped pitted dates
⅓ cup apple juice or apple cider
½ cup butter
⅔ cup granulated sugar
⅔ cup packed brown sugar
1½ teaspoons apple pie spice
½ teaspoon baking soda
¼ teaspoon salt
1 egg
2¼ cups all-purpose flour
¾ cup shredded apple
⅔ cup chopped hickory nuts or black walnuts (optional)
Apple-Cream Cheese Frosting

In a small mixing bowl stir together the raisins, apricots, or dates and apple juice or cider. Let stand for 15 minutes. Drain fruit, reserving liquid. Grease a cookie sheet. Set aside.

In a large mixing bowl beat the butter with an electric mixer on medium to high speed for 30 seconds. Add the granulated sugar, brown sugar, apple pie spice, baking soda, and salt; beat till combined. Beat in the egg and the reserved liquid. Beat in as much of the flour as you can with the mixer. Stir in the remaining flour, the raisin mixture, shredded apple, and, if desired, hickory nuts or black walnuts.

Drop dough by a rounded teaspoon about 2 inches apart onto prepared cookie sheet. Bake in a 375° oven for 9 to 11 minutes or till edges are lightly browned. Cool on cookie sheet for 1 minute. Transfer to a wire rack; cool. Frost cookies with Apple-Cream Cheese Frosting. Store cookies in an airtight container in the refrigerator. Makes about 48 cookies.

Apple-Cream Cheese Frosting: In a medium mixing bowl combine one 3-ounce package softened *cream cheese*, ¼ cup softened *butter*, and 1 teaspoon *vanilla*. Beat with an electric mixer on medium to high speed till fluffy. Gradually beat in 1 cup sifted *powdered sugar*, beating well. Gradually beat in 1¾ cups additional sifted *powdered sugar* and enough *apple juice* or *apple cider* (2 to 3 tablespoons) to make a frosting of spreading consistency.

Nutrition information per cookie: 105 calories, 1 g protein, 18 g carbohydrate, 4 g fat (2 g saturated), 14 mg cholesterol, 61 mg sodium.

Ultimate Bar Cookies

Crush any leftover bars and sprinkle over ice cream as a topping. (Pictured on the cover and on page 17.)

2 cups all-purpose flour
½ cup packed brown sugar
½ cup butter, softened
1 cup coarsely chopped walnuts
1 3½-ounce jar macadamia nuts, coarsely chopped (1 cup)
1 6-ounce package white baking bars, coarsely chopped (1 cup)
1 cup milk chocolate pieces
¾ cup butter
½ cup packed brown sugar

In a medium bowl beat flour, ½ cup brown sugar, and ½ cup butter with an electric mixer on medium speed till mixture forms fine crumbs. Press into the bottom of an ungreased 13x9x2-inch baking pan. Bake in a 350° oven about 15 minutes or till lightly browned.

Transfer pan to a wire rack. Sprinkle nuts, baking bars, and milk chocolate pieces over hot crust. Cook and stir ¾ cup butter and ½ cup brown sugar till bubbly. Cook and stir for 1 minute more. Pour over nuts and chocolate in pan. Bake about 15 minutes more or just till bubbly around edges. Cool in pan on a wire rack. Cut into desired shapes. Makes 36 bars.

Nutrition information per bar: 188 calories, 2 g protein, 16 g carbohydrate, 13 g fat (6 g saturated), 18 mg cholesterol, 12 mg sodium.

Mocha Brownies

These buttery mocha brownies boast plenty of semisweet chocolate and a delightful hint of tangerine.

⅔ cup butter
⅓ cup unsweetened cocoa powder
1 teaspoon instant coffee crystals
1 cup granulated sugar
2 eggs
1 teaspoon vanilla
¾ cup all-purpose flour
½ cup semisweet chocolate pieces or chopped semisweet chocolate
1 teaspoon finely shredded tangerine or orange peel
Sifted powdered sugar (optional)

Grease an 8x8x2-inch baking pan. Set aside. In a medium saucepan melt butter. Stir in cocoa powder and coffee crystals. Remove from heat. Stir in the granulated sugar. Stir in eggs, one at a time, and vanilla. Beat lightly by hand just till combined. Stir in flour. Stir in chocolate pieces and shredded peel.

Spread into prepared pan. Bake in a 350° oven for 30 minutes. Cool in pan on a wire rack. If desired, top with powdered sugar. Cut into bars. Makes 24.

Nutrition information per brownie: 123 calories, 1 g protein, 13 g carbohydrate, 7 g fat (2 g saturated), 24 mg cholesterol, 52 mg sodium.

Creamy, Fudgy, Nutty Brownies

The creamy crown on these brownies is essentially a chocolate cheesecake mixture, so store them in the refrigerator. (Also pictured on the cover.)

4 ounces unsweetened chocolate, chopped
½ cup butter
1 cup all-purpose flour
½ cup chopped walnuts or pecans, toasted
¼ teaspoon baking powder
1½ cups sugar
3 eggs
1 teaspoon vanilla
3 ounces semisweet chocolate, chopped
2 3-ounce packages cream cheese, softened
¼ cup sugar
1 egg
1 tablespoon milk
½ teaspoon vanilla

Grease and lightly flour an 8x8x2-inch baking pan. Set aside. In a small saucepan heat the unsweetened chocolate and butter till melted, stirring occasionally. Remove from heat. Cool slightly. In a medium bowl stir together flour, nuts, and baking powder. Set aside.

In a large mixing bowl stir together melted chocolate mixture and 1½ cups sugar. Add the 3 eggs and the 1 teaspoon vanilla. Using a wooden spoon, lightly beat mixture just till combined (don't overbeat or brownies will rise too high then fall). Stir in flour mixture.

Spread the batter in prepared pan. Bake in a 350° oven for 40 minutes.

Meanwhile, for topping, in a heavy small saucepan heat the semisweet chocolate over low heat till melted, stirring constantly. Cool slightly. In a medium mixing bowl beat the melted semisweet chocolate, softened cream cheese, the ¼ cup sugar, 1 egg, milk, and ½ teaspoon vanilla till combined.

Carefully spread topping evenly over hot brownies. Bake about 10 minutes more or till topping appears set. Cool in pan on a wire rack. Cover and chill at least 2 hours before serving. Cut into bars. Cover and store in the refrigerator. Makes 12 brownies.

Nutrition information per brownie: 409 calories, 7 g protein, 43 g carbohydrate, 27 g fat (9 g saturated), 97 mg cholesterol, 143 mg sodium.

Ultimate Bar Cookies (see recipe, page 15)
and Creamy, Fudgy, Nutty Brownies

Lemon Bars Deluxe

This recipe makes a big batch of these tangy lemon treats so you have plenty to serve hungry guests.

2 cups all-purpose flour
½ cup sifted powdered sugar
1 cup butter
4 eggs
1½ cups granulated sugar
1 to 2 teaspoons finely shredded
    lemon peel (set aside)
⅓ cup lemon juice
¼ cup all-purpose flour
½ teaspoon baking powder
    Sifted powdered sugar (optional)

In a medium mixing bowl stir together 2 cups flour and ½ cup powdered sugar. Using a pastry blender, cut in the butter till mixture clings together. Press into the bottom of an ungreased 13x9x2-inch baking pan.

Bake in a 350° oven for 20 to 25 minutes or till crust is lightly browned.

Meanwhile, in a medium mixing bowl beat together the eggs, granulated sugar, and lemon juice. In a small mixing bowl combine ¼ cup flour and baking powder. Stir the flour mixture and lemon peel into egg mixture. Pour over the baked crust.

Bake for 25 minutes more. Cool in pan on a wire rack. If desired, top with additional powdered sugar. Cut into bars or into 2x1¾-inch diamonds. Cover and store in the refrigerator. Makes 30 bars.

Nutrition information per bar: 141 calories, 2 g protein, 19 g carbohydrate, 7 g fat (4 g saturated), 45 mg cholesterol, 77 mg sodium.

Bar Cookie Magic

If bar cookies play tricks on you by sticking to the pan, line the pan with foil. It may save you cleanup time, too. Tear off a piece of foil bigger than the pan. Press it into the pan, extending it over the pan edges slightly. If a recipe calls for a greased pan, grease the foil. Spread the dough evenly in the pan. Bake and cool the bars in the pan, then use the foil to lift out the bars.

Chocolate-Covered Cherry Cookies

What a neat trick: These cookies are frosted before they're baked! Under the frosting hides a plump, red cherry.

1½ cups all-purpose flour
½ cup unsweetened cocoa powder
1 10-ounce jar maraschino cherries (42 to 48)
½ cup butter
1 cup sugar
¼ teaspoon baking soda
¼ teaspoon baking powder
¼ teaspoon salt
1 egg
1½ teaspoons vanilla
1 6-ounce package (1 cup) semisweet chocolate pieces
½ cup sweetened condensed milk

Combine the flour and cocoa powder. Set aside. Drain the maraschino cherries, reserving juice. Place cherries on paper towels to drain thoroughly. Set aside.

In a large mixing bowl beat butter with an electric mixer on medium to high speed for 30 seconds. Add the sugar, baking soda, baking powder, and salt; beat till combined. Beat in egg and vanilla till combined. Gradually beat in the flour mixture.

Shape dough into 1-inch balls. Place on an ungreased cookie sheet. Press your thumb into the center of each ball. Place a cherry in each center.

For frosting, in a small saucepan combine chocolate pieces and sweetened condensed milk. Cook and stir till chocolate is melted. Stir in 4 teaspoons of the reserved cherry juice.

Spoon about 1 teaspoon of the frosting over each cherry, spreading to cover cherry. (If necessary, thin frosting with additional cherry juice.)

Bake in a 350° oven about 10 minutes or till edges are firm. Cool on cookie sheet for 1 minute. Transfer to a wire rack; cool. Makes 42 to 48 cookies.

Nutrition information per cookie: 98 calories, 1 g protein, 15 g carbohydrate, 4 g fat (2 g saturated), 12 mg cholesterol, 51 mg sodium.

Cranberry-Pecan Tassies

Fruit- and nut-filled tassies—old Scottish for "little cups"—dress up the after-dinner plate with their special-occasion flavor and homestyle comfort.

½ cup butter, softened
1 3-ounce package cream cheese, softened
1 cup all-purpose flour
1 egg
¾ cup packed brown sugar
1 teaspoon vanilla
   Dash salt
⅓ cup finely chopped cranberries
3 tablespoons chopped pecans

For pastry, in a medium mixing bowl beat the butter and cream cheese with an electric mixer on medium to high speed till combined. Stir in the flour. If desired, chill the pastry for 1 hour.

Shape the pastry into 24 balls. Place in ungreased 1¾-inch muffin cups. Press pastry evenly against the bottom and up the side of each muffin cup.

For filling, in another medium mixing bowl beat together the egg, brown sugar, vanilla, and salt just till smooth. Stir in the cranberries and pecans. Spoon the filling into the pastry-lined muffin cups.

Bake in a 325° oven for 30 to 35 minutes or till pastry is golden brown. Cool in muffin cups on wire racks. Remove tassies from muffin cups by running a knife around the edges. Makes 24 tassies.

Nutrition information per tassie: 94 calories, 1 g protein, 10 g carbohydrate, 6 g fat (3 g saturated), 23 mg cholesterol, 59 mg sodium.

Swirled Mint Cookies

Dress up this spectacular cookie for the holiday season by dipping the pressing glass into colored sugar crystals instead of granulated sugar.

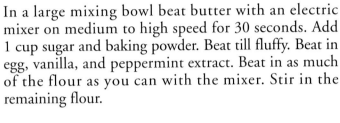

1 cup butter
1 cup sugar
½ teaspoon baking powder
1 egg
1 teaspoon vanilla
½ teaspoon peppermint extract
2 cups all-purpose flour
10 drops red food coloring
10 drops green food coloring
Sugar

In a large mixing bowl beat butter with an electric mixer on medium to high speed for 30 seconds. Add 1 cup sugar and baking powder. Beat till fluffy. Beat in egg, vanilla, and peppermint extract. Beat in as much of the flour as you can with the mixer. Stir in the remaining flour.

Divide dough into 3 equal portions. Stir red food coloring into one portion, stir green food coloring into a second portion, and leave third portion plain. Cover each portion with foil or plastic wrap and chill about 1 hour or till easy to handle.

Divide each color of dough into 4 equal portions. On a lightly floured surface, roll each portion into a ½-inch-diameter rope. Place a red, a green, and a plain rope side by side. Twist together. Repeat with the remaining ropes. Chill twisted ropes for 30 minutes.

Cut the ropes into ½-inch slices for larger cookies or ¼-inch slices for smaller ones. Carefully roll into balls, blending colors as little as possible. Place balls about 2 inches apart on an ungreased cookie sheet. Using a glass dipped in additional sugar, flatten each ball of dough to ¼-inch thickness.

Bake in a 375° oven for 8 to 10 minutes for larger cookies (6 to 8 minutes for smaller ones) or till edges are set. Transfer cookies to a wire rack; cool. Makes about 72 large cookies or about 144 small cookies.

Nutrition information per large cookie: 46 calories, 0 g protein, 5 g carbohydrate, 3 g fat (2 g saturated), 10 mg cholesterol, 29 mg sodium.

Austrian Cookie Tarts

Inspired by an Austrian sandwich cookie, these two-tone sweets get more delicious with a few days' aging.

Browned Butter Spice Dough
Plain Butter Dough
½ cup raspberry or apricot preserves
Sifted powdered sugar

Prepare the Browned Butter Spice Dough and Plain Butter Dough. Wrap and chill for 1 hour. On a lightly floured surface, roll each dough to ⅛-inch thickness. Using 2½- to 3-inch scalloped cookie cutters, cut dough into shapes. (Cut matching shapes from each dough.) Using ½-inch aspic cutters, cut 3 or 4 shapes from center of each plain cutout (do not make cutouts in spice dough). Place on an ungreased cookie sheet.

Bake in a 375° oven for 7 to 8 minutes or till edges are very lightly browned. Transfer to a wire rack; cool.

To assemble, spread about 1 teaspoon preserves on bottom of each spice cookie. Top each with a plain cookie, bottom side down. Just before serving, top with powdered sugar. Makes about 20 cookies.

Browned Butter Spice Dough: Heat ½ cup *butter* over medium heat till the color of light brown sugar. Pour into a medium bowl. Chill till butter resolidifies. Beat browned butter with electric mixer on medium to high speed till softened. Add ½ cup sifted *powdered sugar,* 1 *egg yolk,* 1 teaspoon *vanilla,* ¼ teaspoon ground *cinnamon,* ⅛ teaspoon *salt,* and ⅛ teaspoon ground *cloves.* Beat till fluffy. Beat in as much of ¾ cup *all-purpose flour* as you can with a mixer. Stir in any remaining flour.

Plain Butter Dough: Beat ½ cup *butter* with electric mixer till softened. Beat in ½ cup sifted *powdered sugar,* 1 *egg yolk,* 1 teaspoon *vanilla,* and ⅛ teaspoon *salt.* Beat in as much of 1¼ cups *all-purpose flour* as you can with a mixer. Stir in any remaining flour.

Nutrition information per cookie: 173 calories, 2 g protein, 20 g carbohydrate, 10 g fat (6 g saturated), 46 mg cholesterol, 141 mg sodium.

Peanut Butter Sandwich Cookies

A peanutty fudge filling is a delicious surprise layered between two peanut butter cookies.

½ cup shortening
½ cup peanut butter
½ cup granulated sugar
½ cup packed brown sugar
¾ teaspoon baking soda
1 egg
2 tablespoons milk
1¾ cups all-purpose flour
Fudge Filling

In a medium mixing bowl beat shortening and peanut butter with an electric mixer on medium to high speed for 30 seconds. Add granulated sugar, brown sugar, and baking soda; beat till combined.

Beat in egg and milk till combined. Beat in as much of the flour as you can with the mixer. Stir in remaining flour. Divide dough in half. Wrap each half in waxed paper or plastic wrap and chill for 1 to 2 hours or till easy to handle.

On a lightly floured surface, roll each half of dough to ⅛-inch thickness. Using a 2-inch scalloped round cookie cutter, cut dough into circles. Place cookies about 1 inch apart on an ungreased cookie sheet.

Bake in a 375° oven about 8 minutes or till lightly browned. Transfer cookies to a wire rack; cool.

To assemble, spread the bottoms of half of the cookies with Fudge Filling, using about 1 tablespoon filling on each cookie. Top each with another cookie, bottom side down. Cover and store in the refrigerator. Makes about 25 cookies.

Fudge Filling: In a small saucepan heat 12 ounces *semisweet chocolate* over low heat till melted, stirring constantly. Remove from heat. Stir in 1½ cups dairy *sour cream* and ¾ cup finely chopped *peanuts*. Cool (mixture will stiffen as it cools).

Nutrition information per cookie: 251 calories, 5 g protein, 25 g carbohydrate, 16 g fat (6 g saturated), 15 mg cholesterol, 94 mg sodium.

Sesame Pecan Wafers

Serve these nutty, Southern-style wafers as a complement to a generous scoop of your favorite ice cream.

1 cup butter
⅔ cup sugar
1 teaspoon vanilla
1¾ cups all-purpose flour
½ cup sesame seed
½ cup ground pecans or almonds
2 ounces semisweet chocolate
½ teaspoon shortening

In a large mixing bowl beat butter with an electric mixer on medium to high speed for 30 seconds. Add the sugar and vanilla; beat till combined.

Beat in as much of the flour as you can with the mixer. Stir in the remaining flour, the sesame seed, and ground pecans or almonds.

Divide dough in half. If dough is too sticky to handle, wrap each half in waxed paper or plastic wrap and chill about 1 hour or till easy to handle.

On a lightly floured surface, roll each half of the dough to ⅛-inch thickness. Using 2-inch cookie cutters, cut dough into desired shapes. Place cookies about 1 inch apart on an ungreased cookie sheet.

Bake in a 375° oven for 7 to 8 minutes or till edges are lightly browned. Transfer cookies to a wire rack; cool.

In a heavy small saucepan combine the semisweet chocolate and shortening. Heat over low heat till melted, stirring occasionally. Drizzle chocolate mixture over cookies. Let cookies stand till chocolate is set. Makes about 56 cookies.

Nutrition information per cookie: 70 calories, 1 g protein, 6 g carbohydrate, 5 g fat (2 g saturated), 9 mg cholesterol, 34 mg sodium.

Joe Froggers

Whether so-named because they were as big as the lily pads on Uncle Joe's pond—or from a corruption of "grogger," slang for a rum drinker—the origins of this spice cookie's name are lost in time. Lucky for us the recipe wasn't.

¾ cup butter
1 cup sugar
1½ teaspoons ground ginger
1 teaspoon baking soda
½ teaspoon ground cloves
½ teaspoon ground nutmeg
¼ teaspoon ground allspice
1 cup molasses
2 tablespoons water
2 tablespoons rum or milk
4 cups all-purpose flour

Not Great

Grease a cookie sheet. Set aside. In a large mixing bowl beat butter with an electric mixer on medium to high speed for 30 seconds. Add the sugar, ginger, baking soda, cloves, nutmeg, and allspice; beat till combined.

Beat in the molasses, water, and rum or milk till combined. Beat in as much of the flour as you can with the mixer. Stir in remaining flour. Divide dough in half. Wrap each half in waxed paper or plastic wrap and chill at least 3 hours or till easy to handle.

On a lightly floured surface, roll each half of the dough to about ¼-inch thickness. Using a 4-inch round cookie cutter, cut dough into circles. Place on the prepared cookie sheet.

Bake in a 375° oven for 9 to 11 minutes or till edges are firm and bottoms are just lightly browned. Cool on cookie sheet for 1 minute. Transfer cookies to a wire rack; cool. Makes about 24 cookies.

Nutrition information per cookie: 199 calories, 2 g protein, 0 g carbohydrate, 6 g fat (1 g saturated), 31 mg cholesterol, 88 mg sodium.

Spiral Cookies

Make the dough for these whimsical pink-and-white spirals and chill it overnight. When company comes, just slice and bake them while you're making tea. You'll have pretty cookies to serve warm from the oven.

1 cup butter
1½ cups sugar
1½ teaspoons baking powder
½ teaspoon salt
1 egg
1 teaspoon vanilla
½ teaspoon peppermint extract
   (optional)
2½ cups all-purpose flour
   Red paste food coloring

In a large mixing bowl beat butter with an electric mixer on medium to high speed for 30 seconds. Add the sugar, baking powder, and salt; beat till combined. Beat in the egg, vanilla, and, if desired peppermint extract till combined. Beat in as much of the flour as you can with the mixer. Stir in the remaining flour.

Divide dough in half. Tint one portion of the dough with paste food coloring. Knead coloring into dough till well mixed. If dough is too sticky to handle, wrap each half in waxed paper or plastic wrap and chill about 1 hour or till easy to handle.

On a lightly floured surface, roll each color of dough into a 12x8-inch rectangle. Using a large spatula and your hands, place one rectangle on top of the other. Press down gently with your hands to seal. Starting from a long side, tightly roll up jelly-roll style. Wrap the dough in waxed paper or plastic wrap. Chill at least 2 hours or till firm.

Using a sharp knife, cut log into ¼-inch slices. Place slices about 1 inch apart on an ungreased cookie sheet. Bake in a 375° oven for 8 to 10 minutes or till edges are firm and lightly browned.

Cool on cookie sheet for 1 minute. Transfer cookies to a wire rack; cool. Makes about 48 cookies.

Nutrition information per cookie: *81 calories, 1 g protein, 11 g carbohydrate, 4 g fat (2 g saturated), 15 mg cholesterol, 63 mg sodium.*

Banana Cake with Penuche Frosting

For a combination that's hard to beat, frost this easy-to-make cake right in the pan with the creamy brown sugar frosting.

2½ cups all-purpose flour
1½ cups granulated sugar
1½ teaspoons baking powder
 1 teaspoon baking soda
 ½ teaspoon salt
 1 cup mashed ripe bananas (about 3 bananas)
 ⅔ cup buttermilk or sour milk
 ½ cup shortening
 1 teaspoon vanilla
 2 eggs
    Penuche Frosting
    Chopped nuts (optional)

Grease a 13x9x2-inch baking pan. Set aside. In a large mixing bowl combine flour, 1½ cups sugar, baking powder, baking soda, and salt. Add the bananas, buttermilk or sour milk, shortening, and vanilla.

Beat with an electric mixer on low speed till combined. Add eggs. Beat on medium speed for 2 minutes. Pour into the prepared pan.

Bake in a 350° oven about 35 minutes or till a wooden toothpick inserted near the center comes out clean. Cool completely in pan on a wire rack.

Frost with Penuche Frosting. If desired, immediately sprinkle with chopped nuts. Makes 12 to 16 servings.

Penuche Frosting: In a medium saucepan melt ⅓ cup *butter* over medium heat. Stir in ⅔ cup packed *brown sugar.* Cook and stir till bubbly. Remove from heat. Add 3 tablespoons *milk,* beating vigorously till smooth. By hand, beat in enough sifted *powdered sugar* (about 2½ cups) to make a frosting of spreading consistency. Frost cake immediately.

Nutrition information per serving: 470 calories, 4 g protein, 82 g carbohydrate, 15 g fat (6 g saturated), 50 mg cholesterol, 274 mg sodium.

Busy-Day Cake

No time to bake? Stir up this one-bowl cake in only minutes with easy-to-keep-on-hand ingredients.
Another time, skip the topping and serve it with fresh fruit and whipped cream.

1⅓ cups all-purpose flour
⅔ cup granulated sugar
2 teaspoons baking powder
⅔ cup milk
¼ cup butter, softened
1 egg
1 teaspoon vanilla
  Broiled Coconut Topping

Grease and flour an 8x1½-inch round baking pan. Set aside. In a large mixing bowl combine the flour, ⅔ cup sugar, and baking powder. Add the milk, butter, egg, and vanilla.

Beat with an electric mixer on low speed for 30 seconds. Beat on medium speed for 1 minute. Pour the batter into the prepared pan.

Bake in a 350° oven for 25 to 30 minutes or till a wooden toothpick inserted near the center comes out clean. Remove from heat.

Spread Broiled Coconut Topping over warm cake. Broil about 4 inches from the heat for 3 to 4 minutes or till topping is golden brown. Cool slightly in pan on a wire rack. Serve warm. Makes 8 servings.

Broiled Coconut Topping: In a medium bowl stir together ¼ cup packed *brown sugar* and 2 tablespoons softened *butter*. Stir in 1 tablespoon *milk*. Stir in ½ cup flaked *coconut*, and, if desired, ¼ cup chopped *nuts*.

Nutrition information per serving: 281 calories, 4 g protein, 42 g carbohydrate, 11 g fat (6 g saturated), 51 mg cholesterol, 128 mg sodium.

Apple Cake

Generously rippled with apple slices and cinnamon and drizzled with powdered sugar icing, this luscious cake is especially welcome for breakfast or brunch on crisp autumn mornings.

¼ cup granulated sugar
2 tablespoons all-purpose flour
1½ teaspoons ground cinnamon
5 cups sliced, peeled cooking apples
2½ cups all-purpose flour
1½ cups granulated sugar
1½ teaspoons baking powder
½ teaspoon baking soda
1 cup cooking oil
4 eggs
¼ cup orange juice
2 teaspoons vanilla
   Powdered Sugar Icing (see recipe, page 8)

Grease and lightly flour a 10-inch fluted tube pan. Set aside. In a large mixing bowl combine ¼ cup sugar, 2 tablespoons flour, and cinnamon. Add apples; toss gently to coat. Set aside.

In another large mixing bowl combine 2½ cups flour, 1½ cups sugar, baking powder, and baking soda. Add oil, eggs, orange juice, and vanilla. Beat with an electric mixer on low to medium speed for 30 seconds. Beat on medium speed for 2 minutes.

Pour one-third of the batter (about 1½ cups) into the prepared pan. Top with half of the apple mixture. Spoon another one-third of the batter over apples in pan; top with the remaining apple mixture. Spoon the remaining batter over apples.

Bake in a 350° oven about 1¼ hours or till a wooden toothpick inserted near the center comes out clean.

Cool in pan on a wire rack for 15 minutes. Remove from pan. Cool completely on wire rack. Drizzle with Powdered Sugar Icing. Let cake stand for 1 to 2 hours before slicing. Makes 16 servings.

Nutrition information per serving: 338 calories, 4 g protein, 48 g carbohydrate, 15 g fat (2 g saturated), 53 mg cholesterol, 56 mg sodium.

Oatmeal Cake

The natural goodness of rolled oats together with brown sugar and cinnamon gives this old-fashioned cake its wonderful flavor.

1¼ cups boiling water
1 cup rolled oats
2 cups all-purpose flour
2 teaspoons baking powder
¾ teaspoon ground cinnamon
½ teaspoon baking soda
½ teaspoon salt
¼ teaspoon ground nutmeg
½ cup butter, softened
¾ cup granulated sugar
½ cup packed brown sugar
1 teaspoon vanilla
2 eggs
   Broiled Nut Topping

Grease and lightly flour a 9-inch springform pan. Set aside. Pour boiling water over oats; stir till combined. Let stand for 20 minutes. Combine the flour, baking powder, cinnamon, soda, salt, and nutmeg. Set aside.

In a large mixing bowl beat butter with an electric mixer on medium to high speed for 30 seconds. Add granulated sugar, brown sugar, and vanilla; beat till combined. Add eggs, one at a time, beating well after each. Alternately add flour mixture and oat mixture, beating on low to medium speed after each addition just till combined. Pour the batter into prepared pan.

Bake in a 350° oven for 40 to 45 minutes or till a wooden toothpick inserted near the center comes out clean. Cool in pan on a wire rack for 20 minutes. Remove side of pan; cool cake on rack at least 1 hour.

Transfer cake to a baking sheet. Spread Broiled Nut Topping over warm cake. Broil about 4 inches from the heat for 2 to 3 minutes or till topping is bubbly and golden brown. Cool on wire rack before serving. Makes 12 servings.

Broiled Nut Topping: In a saucepan combine ¼ cup *butter* and 2 tablespoons *half-and-half, light cream,* or *milk.* Cook and stir over medium heat till butter is melted. Add ½ cup packed *brown sugar;* stir till sugar is dissolved. Remove from heat. Stir in ¾ cup chopped *pecans* or *walnuts* and ⅓ cup flaked *coconut.*

Nutrition information per serving: 388 calories, 5 g protein, 52 g carbohydrate, 18 g fat (9 g saturated), 67 mg cholesterol, 296 mg sodium.

Double Fudge Cake

Served right from the pan, this fudgy cocoa cake topped with an even fudgier chocolate frosting, is sure to be a hit at picnics, potlucks, and any other event that calls for casual dining.

2¼ cups all-purpose flour
½ cup unsweetened cocoa powder
1½ teaspoons baking soda
1 teaspoon salt
½ cup shortening
1 cup sugar
1 teaspoon vanilla
3 egg yolks
1⅓ cups cold water
3 egg whites
¾ cup sugar
Fudge Frosting

Grease a 13x9x2-inch baking pan. Set aside. Combine flour, cocoa powder, baking soda, and salt. Set aside.

In a large mixing bowl beat shortening with an electric mixer on medium to high speed for 30 seconds. Add 1 cup sugar and vanilla; beat till combined. Add the egg yolks, one at a time, beating well after each. Alternately add flour mixture and water, beating on low to medium speed after each addition just till combined. Thoroughly wash beaters.

In another large mixing bowl beat egg whites on medium to high speed till soft peaks form (tips curl). Gradually add ¾ cup sugar, about 2 tablespoons at a time, beating till stiff peaks form (tips stand straight). Fold 2 cups of the cocoa batter into egg white mixture to lighten. Gently fold the cocoa-egg white mixture back into remaining batter till combined. Pour batter into the prepared pan.

Bake in a 350° oven about 40 minutes or till a wooden toothpick inserted near the center comes out clean. Cool completely in pan on a wire rack. Frost with Fudge Frosting. Makes 12 servings.

Fudge Frosting: In a medium saucepan combine one 5-ounce can *evaporated milk,* ½ cup *sugar,* and 2 tablespoons *butter.* Cook and stir over medium heat till boiling. Boil for 5 minutes, stirring occasionally. Remove from heat. Stir in 1½ cups *semisweet chocolate pieces* till melted. Stir in 1 tablespoon light-colored *corn syrup.* Use immediately.

Nutrition information per serving: 471 calories, 7 g protein, 72 g carbohydrate, 19 g fat (4 g saturated), 62 mg cholesterol, 389 mg sodium.

Upside-Down Pineapple-Orange Cake

For a twist on pineapple upside-down cake, we added mandarin oranges, using half a can of pineapple slices and half a can of orange sections. If you prefer to make the cake with just one fruit, use a whole can.

⅔ cup packed brown sugar
6 tablespoons butter
1½ teaspoons finely shredded orange peel
1 11-ounce can mandarin orange sections
1 8-ounce can pineapple slices
1⅓ cups all-purpose flour
1¼ teaspoons baking powder
½ teaspoon salt
6 tablespoons butter
1 cup granulated sugar
¼ teaspoon almond extract
2 eggs
⅔ cup dairy sour cream
  Sweetened Whipped Cream (optional)

In a saucepan combine brown sugar, 6 tablespoons butter, and orange peel. Cook and stir over medium heat till mixture is bubbly. Pour into an ungreased 9x9x2-inch baking pan.

Drain the oranges and pineapple. Cut half of the pineapple slices in half. Arrange the half slices of pineapple and half of the orange sections in pan. (Reserve remaining oranges and pineapple for another use.) Combine flour, baking powder, and salt.

In a large mixing bowl beat 6 tablespoons butter with an electric mixer on medium to high speed for 30 seconds. Add granulated sugar and almond extract; beat till combined. Add eggs, one at a time, beating well after each. Alternately add flour mixture and sour cream, beating on low to medium speed after each addition just till combined. Spoon over fruit.

Bake in a 350° oven for 35 to 40 minutes or till a wooden toothpick inserted near the center comes out clean. Cool in pan on a wire rack for 5 minutes. Invert onto a serving plate. Serve warm. If desired, top with Sweetened Whipped Cream. Makes 8 servings.

Sweetened Whipped Cream: In a chilled medium bowl combine 1 cup *whipping cream*, 2 tablespoons *granulated sugar*, and ½ teaspoon *vanilla*. Beat with an electric mixer on medium to high speed till soft peaks form (tips curl).

Nutrition information per serving: 455 calories, 4 g protein, 64 g carbohydrate, 21 g fat (12 g saturated), 107 mg cholesterol, 371 mg sodium.

Chocolate Cream Cake

This trio of devil's food layers is first filled with vanilla butter cream and then the entire cake is swirled with chocolatey cream cheese frosting—an irresistible combination!

2⅔ cups all-purpose flour
1½ teaspoons baking soda
¾ teaspoon salt
¾ cup butter
2¼ cups granulated sugar
2 teaspoons vanilla
3 eggs
3 ounces unsweetened chocolate, melted and cooled
1½ cups ice water
Butter Cream Filling
Chocolate-Cream Cheese Frosting

Grease and lightly flour three 9x1½- or 8x1½-inch round baking pans. Combine flour, soda, and salt.

In a large mixing bowl beat the butter with an electric mixer on medium to high speed for 30 seconds. Add 2¼ cups sugar and vanilla; beat till combined. Add eggs, one at a time, beating well after each. Beat in chocolate. Alternately add flour mixture and water, beating on low to medium speed after each addition just till combined. Pour into prepared pans.

Bake in a 350° oven for 25 to 30 minutes or till a wooden toothpick inserted near the centers comes out clean. Cool in pans on wire racks for 10 minutes. Remove from pans. Cool completely on wire racks.

Spread Butter Cream Filling on two of the layers; stack layers. Top with remaining layer. Frost cake with Chocolate-Cream Cheese Frosting. Cover and store in the refrigerator. Makes 12 servings.

Butter Cream Filling: Beat ½ cup *butter* till softened. Beat in 2¼ cups sifted *powdered sugar,* 2 tablespoons *milk,* and ½ teaspoon *vanilla.* Beat in additional *milk,* if necessary, to make a filling of spreading consistency.

Chocolate-Cream Cheese Frosting: Beat ½ of an 8-ounce package *cream cheese* till softened. Beat in 3 tablespoons *milk.* Beat in 3¾ cups sifted *powdered sugar.* Beat in 3 ounces *unsweetened chocolate,* melted and cooled, and 1 teaspoon *vanilla.* Beat in additional *milk,* if necessary, to make of spreading consistency.

Nutrition information per serving: 730 calories, 7 g protein, 113 g carbohydrate, 32 g fat (17 g saturated), 115 mg cholesterol, 564 mg sodium.

Chocolate-Raspberry Cake

A cloud of fluffy frosting, tinted pink with raspberry preserves, adorns these light chocolate layers.

1½ cups all-purpose flour
1 cup sugar
1 teaspoon baking powder
½ teaspoon baking soda
½ teaspoon salt
1 cup buttermilk or sour milk
⅓ cup cooking oil
2 egg yolks
2 ounces unsweetened chocolate, melted and cooled
2 egg whites
½ cup sugar
3 tablespoons raspberry liqueur
   Fluffy Raspberry Frosting

Grease and lightly flour two 9x1½-inch round baking pans. Set aside. In a large mixing bowl combine flour, 1 cup sugar, baking powder, baking soda, and salt. Make a well in the center. Add buttermilk or sour milk, oil, egg yolks, and chocolate. Beat with an electric mixer on low to medium speed till combined. Beat on medium to high speed till smooth.

Thoroughly wash beaters. In a medium mixing bowl beat egg whites on medium to high speed till soft peaks form (tips curl). Add ½ cup sugar, 2 tablespoons at a time, beating on medium to high speed till stiff peaks form (tips stand straight). Fold into chocolate mixture. Pour into the prepared pans.

Bake in a 350° oven for 25 to 30 minutes or till tops spring back when lightly touched. Cool in pans on wire racks for 10 minutes. Remove from pans. Cool completely on racks. Brush layers with liqueur. Fill and frost with Fluffy Raspberry Frosting. Serves 12.

Fluffy Raspberry Frosting: Melt ⅓ cup seedless *raspberry preserves*. Keep warm. In top of double boiler combine 1½ cups *sugar*, ⅓ cup *cold water*, 2 *egg whites*, and ¼ teaspoon *cream of tartar* or 2 teaspoons light-colored *corn syrup*. Beat with electric mixer on low speed for 30 seconds. Place over boiling water (upper pan should not touch water). Cook, beating constantly with electric mixer on high speed, for 7 to 9 minutes or till stiff peaks forms (tips stand straight). Beat in preserves and, if desired, 1 or 2 drops *red food coloring*. Remove from heat. Beat for 2 to 3 minutes more or till spreading consistency.

Nutrition information per serving: 381 calories, 4 g protein, 71 g carbohydrate, 10 g fat (2 g saturated), 36 mg cholesterol, 215 mg sodium.

Orange Cake

A velvety chocolate frosting sets off the sunny citrus flavor of this yellow butter cake. If you have any leftover frosting, use it to frost cupcakes.

2¾ cups all-purpose flour
2 teaspoons baking powder
½ teaspoon salt
¼ teaspoon baking soda
½ cup butter
1¾ cups granulated sugar
1 teaspoon vanilla
2 eggs
1 cup milk
2 tablespoons finely shredded orange peel (set aside)
¼ cup orange juice
    Truffle Frosting
    Orange peel shreds (optional)

Grease and flour two 9x1½- or 8x1½-inch round baking pans. Combine flour, baking powder, salt, and baking soda. Set aside. In a large mixing bowl beat butter with an electric mixer on medium to high speed for 30 seconds. Beat in 1¾ cups sugar and vanilla till combined. Add eggs, one at a time, beating well after each. Combine milk and juice. Alternately add flour mixture and milk mixture, beating on low to medium speed after each addition just till combined. Stir in 2 tablespoons peel. Pour into prepared pans.

Bake in a 350° oven for 30 to 35 minutes or till a wooden toothpick inserted near the centers comes out clean. Cool in pans on wire racks for 10 minutes. Remove from pans. Cool completely on wire racks.

Fill and frost cake with Truffle Frosting. If desired, pipe decorative borders around top and bottom of cake and sprinkle cake with orange peel shreds. Cover and store in the refrigerator. Makes 12 servings.

Truffle Frosting: In a heavy medium saucepan bring 3 cups *whipping cream* and ½ cup light-colored *corn syrup* to simmering. Remove from heat. Stir in two 12-ounce packages (4 cups) *semisweet chocolate pieces* and 2 teaspoons *vanilla*. Let stand for 2 minutes. Whisk mixture until smooth and melted. Cover and chill about 1½ hours or till easy to spread, stirring occasionally. Beat with an electric mixer till fluffy.

Nutrition information per serving: 814 calories, 8 g protein, 101 g carbohydrate, 47 g fat (19 g saturated), 139 mg cholesterol, 307 mg sodium.

Coconut-Almond Praline Cake

The frosting for this three-tiered beauty is a cooked one that must be cooled until it's thick enough to spread. To speed the cooling process, set the pan of frosting in a bowl of ice water.

3 cups all-purpose flour
2 teaspoons baking powder
½ teaspoon salt
¼ teaspoon baking soda
½ cup butter
1 cup granulated sugar
1 cup packed brown sugar
1½ teaspoons vanilla
¼ teaspoon almond extract
2 eggs
1½ cups milk
½ cup flaked coconut, toasted
    Coconut-Almond Praline Frosting
    Orange slice twists (optional)

Grease and lightly flour three 9x1½-inch round baking pans. Set aside. Combine flour, baking powder, salt, and baking soda. Set aside.

In a large mixing bowl beat butter with an electric mixer on medium to high speed for 30 seconds. Add granulated sugar, brown sugar, vanilla, and almond extract; beat till combined. Add eggs, one at a time, beating well after each. Alternately add flour mixture and milk, beating on low speed after each addition just till combined. Stir in toasted coconut. Pour batter into the prepared pans.

Bake in a 350° oven about 25 minutes or till a wooden toothpick inserted near the centers comes out clean. Cool in pans on wire racks for 10 minutes. Remove from pans. Cool completely on wire racks. Spread Coconut-Almond Praline Frosting over the top of each layer; stack layers. If desired, garnish with orange twists. Cover and store in the refrigerator. Serves 12.

Coconut-Almond Praline Frosting: In a medium saucepan stir together 1 *egg,* 1 *egg yolk,* and 1 cup *granulated sugar.* Add 1 cup *evaporated milk,* 6 tablespoons *butter,* and ¼ teaspoon *almond extract.* Cook and stir over medium heat about 8 minutes or till thickened and bubbly. Stir in 1 cup *slivered almonds,* toasted and chopped, and ¾ cup *flaked coconut.* Cool till thick enough to spread.

Nutrition information per serving: 583 calories, 10 g protein, 83 g carbohydrate, 25 g fat (12 g saturated), 115 mg cholesterol, 403 mg sodium.

Chocolate Ice Cream Roll with Raspberry Sauce

Make this elegant dessert up to two weeks in advance and store it, tightly wrapped, in your freezer.

⅓ cup all-purpose flour
¼ cup unsweetened cocoa powder
1 teaspoon baking powder
¼ teaspoon salt
4 egg yolks
½ teaspoon vanilla
⅓ cup granulated sugar
4 egg whites
½ cup granulated sugar
  Sifted powdered sugar
1 quart butter almond or chocolate almond ice cream, softened
  Raspberry Sauce
  Raspberries (optional)
  Fresh mint sprigs (optional)

Grease and flour a 15x10x1-inch jelly-roll pan. Stir together flour, cocoa powder, baking powder, and salt. In a small mixing bowl beat egg yolks and vanilla with an electric mixer on high speed about 5 minutes or till thick and lemon-colored. Gradually add ⅓ cup sugar, beating on medium speed about 5 minutes or till sugar is almost dissolved. Thoroughly wash beaters.

In a large mixing bowl beat egg whites on medium to high speed till soft peaks form (tips curl). Gradually add ½ cup sugar, beating till stiff peaks form (tips stand straight). Fold yolk mixture into egg white mixture. Sprinkle flour mixture over egg mixture. Fold in gently, just till combined. Spread into prepared pan.

Bake in a 375° oven for 12 to 15 minutes or till top springs back when lightly touched. Immediately loosen edges of cake. Turn out onto a towel sprinkled with powdered sugar. Starting from a short side, roll up cake and towel together. Cool on a wire rack.

Unroll cake. Spread ice cream on cake to within 1 inch of edges. Reroll cake without towel. Wrap and freeze at least 4 hours. To serve, drizzle Raspberry Sauce over dessert plates. Slice cake and place on plates. If desired, garnish with raspberries and mint. Makes 10 servings.

Raspberry Sauce: In a small saucepan combine ⅔ cup seedless *raspberry preserves,* 1 tablespoon *lemon juice,* and ¼ teaspoon *almond extract.* Cook and stir just till melted. Cool slightly.

Nutrition information per serving: 255 calories, 5 g protein, 44 g carbohydrate, 7 g fat (3 g saturated), 116 mg cholesterol, 138 mg sodium.

Vanilla-Fudge Marble Cake

Although not a true pound cake, this two-toned ring looks and tastes the part. Serve it with ice cream for a sure-to-please dessert.

2¾ cups sifted all-purpose flour
1½ teaspoons baking powder
½ teaspoon baking soda
½ teaspoon salt
¾ cup butter
1½ cups sugar
2 teaspoons vanilla
2 eggs
1¼ cups buttermilk or sour milk
⅔ cup chocolate-flavored syrup
  Semisweet Chocolate Icing

Grease and lightly flour a 10-inch fluted tube pan. Set aside. Combine flour, baking powder, baking soda, and salt. Set aside.

In a large mixing bowl beat the butter with an electric mixer on medium to high speed for 30 seconds. Add sugar and vanilla. Beat till fluffy. Add eggs, one at a time, beating well after each. Alternately add flour mixture and buttermilk or sour milk, beating on low speed after each addition just till combined. Reserve 2 cups of the batter. Pour the remaining batter into the prepared pan.

In a small mixing bowl combine chocolate-flavored syrup and the reserved batter. Beat on low speed till well combined. Pour the chocolate batter over vanilla batter in pan. Do not mix.

Bake in a 350° oven about 50 minutes or till a wooden toothpick inserted near the center comes out clean. Cool in pan on a wire rack for 15 minutes. Remove from pan. Cool completely on wire rack. Drizzle cake with Semisweet Chocolate Icing. Makes 12 servings.

Semisweet Chocolate Icing: In a small saucepan heat ½ cup *semisweet chocolate pieces,* 2 tablespoons *butter,* 1 tablespoon light-colored *corn syrup,* and ¼ teaspoon *vanilla* over low heat till the chocolate is melted and mixture is smooth, stirring constantly. Use immediately.

Nutrition information per serving: 412 calories, 5 g protein, 63 g carbohydrate, 17 g fat (9 g saturated), 72 mg cholesterol, 391 mg sodium.

Daffodil Cake

Celebrate the rites of spring with this classic angel food cake marbled with lemon-yellow sponge cake. It's only fitting to create a simple centerpiece with daffodils from your garden.

1½ cups egg whites (11 or 12 large)
1 cup sifted cake flour or sifted
    all-purpose flour
¾ cup granulated sugar
2 teaspoons vanilla
1½ teaspoons cream of tartar
¼ teaspoon salt
¾ cup granulated sugar
6 egg yolks
1½ teaspoons finely shredded lemon
    peel
Tangy Lemon Frosting
Lemon peel shreds (optional)

In a very large mixing bowl allow egg whites to stand at room temperature for 30 minutes. Meanwhile, sift together flour and ¾ cup sugar 3 times. Set aside. Add vanilla, cream of tartar, and salt to egg whites. Beat with electric mixer on medium to high speed till soft peaks form (tips curl). Gradually add ¾ cup sugar, 2 tablespoons at a time, beating till stiff peaks form (tips stand straight). Sift one-fourth of the flour mixture over egg white mixture; fold in gently. (If too full, transfer to a larger bowl.) Repeat with remaining flour mixture, using one-fourth of the mixture each time. Transfer half of the batter to another bowl.

In a small bowl beat egg yolks on high speed about 6 minutes or till thick and lemon-colored. Fold in 1½ teaspoons lemon peel. Gently fold into half of the white batter. Alternately spoon yellow batter and remaining white batter into an ungreased 10-inch tube pan. Swirl a metal spatula through batters to marble.

Bake on the lowest rack in a 350° oven for 40 to 45 minutes or till top springs back when lightly touched. Immediately invert cake in pan; cool completely. Remove from pan. Place upside down on a plate. Frost with Tangy Lemon Frosting. If desired, sprinkle with lemon peel shreds. Makes 12 servings.

Tangy Lemon Frosting: In a large mixing bowl beat ½ cup *butter* till softened. Beat in 5½ cups sifted *powdered sugar*, ½ teaspoon finely shredded *lemon peel*, and ⅓ cup *lemon juice*. Beat in additional *lemon juice*, if necessary, to make of spreading consistency.

Nutrition information per serving: 424 calories, 5 g protein, 79 g carbohydrate, 10 g fat (5 g saturated), 127 mg cholesterol, 189 mg sodium.

INDEX